SRA
Reading
Mastery®
Transformations

Reading
Workbook B

Siegfried Engelmann

Susie Andrist

Tina Wells

Mc
Graw
Hill

Acknowledgments

The authors are extremely grateful to Tina Wells for keeping the ship afloat on this project, and to Patricia McFadden, Margie Mayo, and Chris Gladfelter for their great attention to detail.

PHOTO CREDITS
(br) Stocktrek Images, Inc./Alamy Stock Photo; (cr) Stocktrek/Brand X Pictures/Getty Images; (l) Nick Norman/National Geographic/Getty Images; (c) Diane Nelson; (r) Amar and Isabelle Guillen - Guillen Photo LLC/Alamy Stock Photo; (inset) taviphoto/iStock/Getty Images

mheducation.com/prek-12

Copyright © 2021 McGraw-Hill Education

Send all inquiries to:
McGraw-Hill Education
8787 Orion Place
Columbus, OH 43240

ISBN: 978-0-07-905369-5
MHID: 0-07-905369-6

Printed in the United States of America.

2 3 4 5 6 7 8 9 10 LMN 26 25 24 23 22 21

A STORY ITEMS

1. The woman in the gray coat said that not many people would be interested in Leonard's invention. Did she really think that? _____

2. Why did she say it?
   - She didn't like the invention.
   - She didn't want to talk to her boss.
   - She didn't want to pay a lot for the invention.

3. The woman in the gray coat made two offers. Tell about her **first** offer.

   _____ dollars for the invention and

   _____ for every copy that is sold

4. Did Leonard like that offer? _____

5. Did Grandmother Esther like that offer? _____

6. Tell about the offer everyone agreed on.

   _____ dollars for the invention and

   _____ for every copy that is sold

7. Circle the 2 ways that tell how the woman in the gray coat changed after she made the deal.
   - Her voice was pleasant.
   - She smiled.
   - She yelled.
   - Her voice was loud.
   - Her voice was higher.
   - She closed her eyes.

8. What did Grandmother Esther and Leonard have to do to finish the deal?
   - win a prize
   - get another patent
   - sign papers

9. Who did Grandmother Esther think would win first prize?

_____

10. Who won first price? _____

11. What was the person's invention? _____

_____

12. How much money did Leonard win for his prize?

_____

13. Why did Leonard want Grandmother Esther to go on the stage with him?
    • She wanted to go up there.
    • She helped with his invention.
    • She knew Ronald Hogan.

14. Did she want to do that? _____

B REVIEW ITEM

15. The picture shows the sun and two balls. Fix up the balls so that half of each ball is in sunlight and half is in shadow.

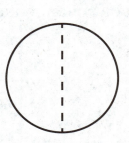  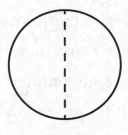

sun

GO TO PART C IN YOUR TEXTBOOK

A STORY ITEMS

1. Name one reason Leonard didn't have much free time anymore.

   _____

2. What name did ABC Home Products give Leonard's invention?

   _____

> **Answer these questions about the ad:**
>
> 3. The ad said you should put a Light Saver in _____ of your house.
>
> 4. Who should you see about getting some Light Savers?
>
>   _____
>
> 5. Leonard's mother solved one problem she had with grocery shopping. She solved that problem by buying ▯ .
>   - a grocery cart
>   - a Mr. Light Saver
>   - an automatic list-writer
>
> 6. Leonard's mother still had a problem when she went grocery shopping. What was her problem?
>   - opening the trunk while holding groceries
>   - turning on lights while holding groceries
>   - holding groceries and playing the drums

1. The woman in the gray coat made two offers. Her first offer was

    _____ dollars for the invention and

    _____ for every copy that is sold.

2. Did Leonard like that offer? _____

3. Did Grandmother Esther like that offer? _____

4. The offer that everyone agreed on was _____

    dollars for the invention and _____ for every copy

    that is sold.

GO TO PART D IN YOUR TEXTBOOK

A **INFORMATION ITEMS**

1. How many suns are in the solar system? _____

2. How many planets are in the solar system? _____

3. Name the planet we live on. _____

4. What's in the middle of the solar system? _____

5. Name the only part of the solar system that's burning.
   • our moon   • Earth   • the sun

6. Is Earth the planet that is closest to the sun? _____

7. The sun gives _____ and _____ to all the planets.

8. Make an **X** on the sun.

9. Make a **Y** on Earth.

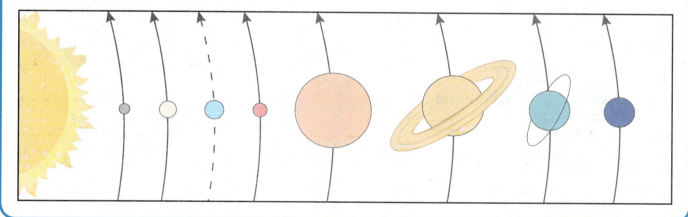

10. The planets are named below with Mercury first and Venus second.

    Fill in the names of the missing planets.

    Mercury, Venus, _____ , Mars,

    _____ , Saturn, _____ , Neptune

11. Which planet is largest? _____

12. Which planet is next-largest? _____

13. How many times larger than Earth is the sun?

    • one hundred   • one thousand   • ten thousand

B STORY ITEMS

1. Does today's story take place in the past, the present, or the future?

   _____

2. Students who do well on the test will go on a trip. Where will they go?

   _____

3. About how many students are taking the test with Wendy?

   _____

4. How many students will go on the trip? _____

5. What country are those students from? _____

6. How long will the test take? _____

7. Why did Wendy feel sick at the end of the chapter? _____

   _____

   _____

GO TO PART D IN YOUR TEXTBOOK

A INFORMATION ITEMS

1. Write the present year on line **C.**

2. Then write **past** or **future** next to each of the other years.

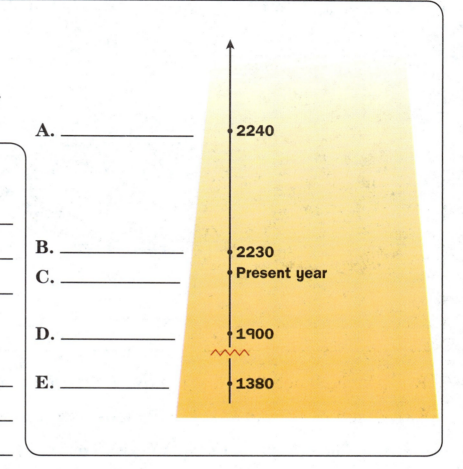

A. _____ • 2240

3. Write any **3** years that are in the past.

_____

_____

_____

B. _____ • 2230
C. _____ • Present year

4. Write any **3** years that are in the future.

D. _____ • 1900

_____

_____

_____

E. _____ • 1380

5. Things that have already happened are in the _____ .

6. Things that are happening now are in the _____ .

7. Things that will happen are in the _____ .

B STORY ITEMS

1. How long is Traveler Four? _____

2. How many people are in the crew? _____

3. How many passengers does it hold? _____

4. How fast can it travel? _____

5. How far is it from Earth to Jupiter?

    • 200 million miles   • 400 thousand miles   • 400 million miles

6. Here's a picture of Traveler Four. Label the lettered parts.

A _____   B _____ **section**

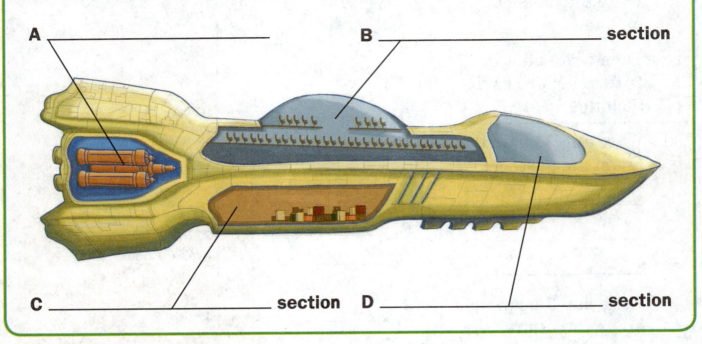

C _____ **section**   D _____ **section**

7. Which planet did Wendy know the most about? _____

8. Which planet did she find the most interesting? _____

9. Why did she think that planet was the most interesting?

_____

C **REVIEW ITEM**

The planets are named below with Mercury first and Venus second.

Write the names of the missing planets.

Mercury, Venus, Earth, _____ , Jupiter,

_____ , Uranus, _____

GO TO PART D IN YOUR TEXTBOOK

A **STORY ITEMS**

Answer these questions about Traveler Four.

1. How many people are in the crew? _____

2. How many passengers does it hold? _____

3. How fast can it travel? _____

4. How long did the test take? _____

5. Was Wendy sure that she had answered all the questions correctly?

_____

6. Name all the Travelers that were earlier than Traveler Four.

_____

7. How fast could Traveler One go? _____

8. The woman told the students how they would find out whether they would go on the trip. How would they find out? _____

_____

9. Write the first name of the girl who sat behind Wendy during the test.

_____

10. Did the girl think she did well on the test? _____

11. What did Wendy do after the math class every day?

_____

12. Was Wendy selected for the trip? _____

13. What planet will she go to? _____

1. Name the planet we live on. _____

2. What's in the middle of the solar system? _____

3. Name the only part of the solar system that's burning. _____

4. Which planet is largest? _____

5. Which planet is next-largest? _____

6. How many moons does Saturn have? _____

7. How many moons does Jupiter have? _____

8. How far is it from Earth to Jupiter?

   • 400 miles   • 400 million miles   • 400 thousand miles

9. The picture shows half a hailstone. How many times did the stone go through a cloud? _____

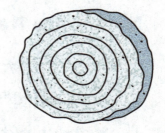

GO TO PART C IN YOUR TEXTBOOK

A INFORMATION ITEMS

1. Which letter shows where Wendy's flight began? _____

2. Which letter shows Tokyo? _____

3. Draw an arrow to show the route that Wendy's jet plane took.

4. What's the largest city in Japan? _____

5. In which direction did the jet fly from Canada to Tokyo? _____

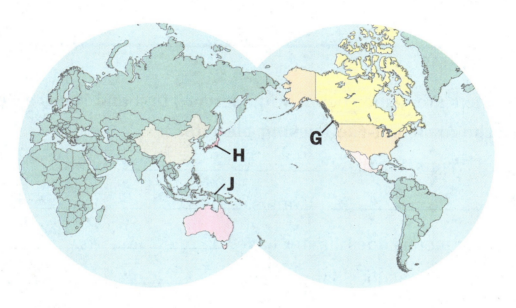

B STORY ITEMS

1. What city could Wendy see from the space station? _____

2. What country is that city in? _____

3. What country did Wendy's jet come from? _____

4. Wendy's baggage could not weigh more than ▨ .

   • 50 pounds   • 100 pounds   • 140 pounds

5. Was Wendy in good health? _____

6. What surprise did Wendy have at the space station?

_____

7. Was Sidney's name on the list of students who were going on the trip?

_____

8. Why did Sidney get to go on the trip?

_____

9. Most of the other passengers were not students. Who were they?

_____

C REVIEW ITEMS

1. The planets are named below with Mercury first and Venus second.
   Write the names of the missing planets.

   Mercury, Venus, Earth, _____, Jupiter,

   _____, Uranus, _____.

2. How many moons does Jupiter have? _____

3. How many moons does Saturn have? _____

4. How far is it from Earth to Jupiter?
   • 800 million miles   • 40 million miles   • 400 million miles

5. If other people want to make copies of an invention, they have to make
   a deal with the _____.

6. What does the inventor usually make those people do?

   _____

GO TO PART D IN YOUR TEXTBOOK

A STORY ITEMS

1. Circle **5** things that were near Wendy's seat.

    - space books
    - space helmet
    - spacesuit
    - space food
    - bed
    - plates
    - writing desk
    - TV screen
    - window

2. Why would everybody need tanks of oxygen when they got to Jupiter?

    _____

    _____

3. How far back did the passengers have to move their seats before they

    took off? _____

4. What was Wendy's idea about why the ship was shaking?

    - It was speeding through layers of air.
    - It was falling apart.
    - It was too old.
    - It was too heavy.

5. The pressure on Wendy felt like _____ sitting on
    her chest.

6. In what part of the spaceship were the engines?

    _____

7. The sound of the engines couldn't reach the passenger section because

    the spaceship _____

    _____ .

8. What planet did Wendy see when she looked out the window?

    _____

9. Make an **X** on a passenger seat.

10. Make a **P** on the spacesuit.

11. Make an **H** on the space helmet.

12. Make a **T** on the window.

13. Make an **R** on the writing desk.

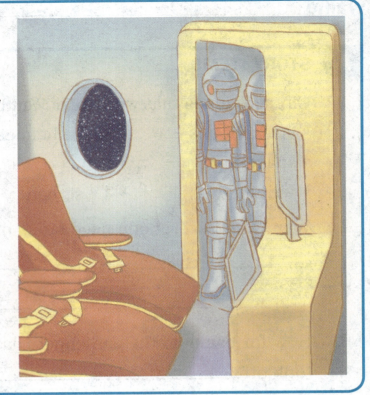

14. What planet is shown in the picture? _____

GO TO PART C IN YOUR TEXTBOOK

A INFORMATION ITEMS

1. Gravity is the force that _____ .

2. If something weighed 100 pounds on Earth, how many pounds would it weigh on the moon? _____

3. If something weighed 20 pounds on Earth, would it weigh more than 20 pounds on Saturn? _____

4. Would it weigh more than 20 pounds on the moon? _____

5. A person weighs 100 pounds on planet A and 300 pounds on planet B. Which planet has stronger gravity? _____

6. A person weighs 100 pounds on planet A and 90 pounds on planet B. Which planet has stronger gravity? _____

7. Planet A has weaker gravity than planet M. On which of those planets would you weigh more? _____

8. Which planets have stronger gravity, the **bigger** planets or the **smaller** ones?

   _____

B STORY ITEMS

1. Why did Earth seem to get smaller? _____

   _____

2. What makes the sky around Earth look blue?
   • a layer of air   • the sun   • a layer of clouds

3. The pilot turned off the engines when the ship was out in space. Did the spaceship slow down? _____

4. Was there any air outside the spaceship? _____

5. What happens to people and things when there's no gravity?
   • They drop.   • They float.   • They survive.

6. When the gravity device is turned on, do things float in the air or fall to the floor? _____

7. The gravity device is off. What would happen if you hit a **big** blob of floating liquid? _____

   _____

8. Do things fall to the floor when the gravity device is off? _____

9. Did the gravity device come back on **fast** or **slowly**? _____

10. If you drop something on Earth, it falls to the ground. What makes it fall?

    _____

C   REVIEW ITEM

Fill in the blanks to show the four seasons.

winter, _____ , summer, fall, _____ ,

spring, _____ , _____

GO TO PART E IN YOUR TEXTBOOK

A STORY ITEMS

1. Traveler Four had gone over 40 million miles in less than ▨▨▨ .
   - 1 hour   - 11 hours   - 1 day

Answer these questions about Earth and Mars.

2. Which planet has more clouds around it? _____

3. Which planet is smaller? _____

4. Which planet is colder? _____

5. Why is that planet colder? _____

   _____

6. Did Wendy sleep well during the first night on the spaceship? _____

7. Why did the sun seem to be getting smaller? _____

   _____

8. Everyone needed to do exercises so they wouldn't get _____ .

9. Name **2** of the exercises they did. _____

   _____

10. How did Wendy sleep the second night? _____

11. What planet did everyone see on the next day? _____

12. What did the pilot do to the spaceship? _____

    _____

13. How many moons of Jupiter could Wendy see?
    - 79   - 72   - 62   - 7

14. How many moons does Jupiter have altogether? _____

15. Which planet has more moons, Saturn or Jupiter? _____

16. Circle the 5 things that tell how Jupiter looked to Wendy.

- It was small.
- It was green and blue.
- It was beautiful.
- It had stripes.

- She could see seven moons.
- It was huge.
- She could see twelve moons.
- It was brown, orange, and white.

B REVIEW ITEMS

1. In which direction do geese migrate in the fall? _____

2. In which direction do geese migrate in the spring? _____

3. Write the directions **north, south, east,** and **west** in the boxes.

4. Make a line that starts at the circle on the map and goes north.

5. If you start at the circle and move to the number 4, in which direction do you go? _____

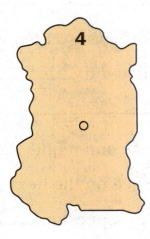

GO TO PART C IN YOUR TEXTBOOK

A **STORY ITEMS—*Little House on the Prairie***

1. Why did Pa pull all the grass in a large circle?
    - to make a big fire
    - so he wouldn't set the prairie on fire
    - to feed the horses

2. What did the horses do while Pa pulled the grass?

    _____

3. Where did they get twigs for the fire? _____

4. What did they eat for supper? _____

5. What did they hear about a half mile away? _____

6. What did Laura think she saw on the other side of the campfire?

    _____

7. Why didn't Pa think she was right?

    _____

8. Who walked toward the eyes? _____

9. Who did the eyes belong to? _____

10. Why didn't Jack eat dinner? _____

11. The title of chapter 3 is ▆▆▆▆ .
    - Going Out
    - Going West
    - Camp on the High Prairie
    - Crossing the Creek

B **STORY ITEMS—*Spaghetti***

1. Where did Gabriel want to live at the beginning of the story?

    _____

2. Where did he actually live? _____

3. What did he hear in the street? _____

4. What did Gabriel name the kitten? _____

5. Why did he give it that name? _____

_____

6. Who did Gabriel think owned the kitten? _____

7. Where did Gabriel take the kitten at the end of the story?

_____

8. Why didn't Gabriel want to live with the coyotes now?

_____

C SETTING, CHARACTERS, PLOT—*Spaghetti*

1. What is the main setting for this story?

_____

2. Name the 2 main characters in this story.

_____

3. Write the plot for this story. Tell about Gabriel. Tell how he felt before he found Spaghetti. Tell what happened to Gabriel. Tell how his feelings changed.

_____

_____

_____

_____

_____

_____

END OF LESSON 60

A STORY ITEMS

1. How much oxygen is on Io? _____

2. What must people wear so they can breathe on Io?

   _____

3. The automatic radio in the spacesuit tells people how to get back to the

   _____ and how much _____ they

   have left.

4. How well did Wendy sleep on the spaceship last night? _____

5. Name the moon where the ship will land. _____

6. What makes it dark on the surface of Jupiter?

   _____

7. Could you see very far on Jupiter with bright lights? _____

8. Do gases surround Io? _____

9. Does Io move around Jupiter **fast** or **slowly?** _____

10. It takes Io about _____ to go all the way around Jupiter.

11. Where did the passengers keep their spacesuits? _____

   _____

12. The passengers tried on their spacesuits. Did the spacesuits feel **heavy**

   or **light?** _____

13. Would they feel that way on Io? _____

14. Tell why. _____

   _____

15. Why did the engines of the spaceship start up again?

   • to slow the ship down

   • to speed the ship up

   • to turn in circles

16. What planet is shown?

   _____

17. Make an **X** on the "eye" of the planet.

18. Which is bigger, the "eye" or Earth?

   _____

19. The planets are named below with Mercury first.
   Write the names of the missing planets.

   Mercury, _____, Earth, _____,

   Jupiter, _____, Uranus, _____.

GO TO PART C IN YOUR TEXTBOOK

A STORY ITEMS

1. As Traveler Four approached Io, the engines came on with great force. Tell why. _____

2. Did Wendy **feel** the engines or **hear** the engines?

   _____

3. Why were the passengers glad to leave the spaceship?

   _____

4. Did Wendy feel **light** or **heavy** when she left the ship?

   _____

5. Tell why.
   • Io has weaker gravity.
   • Io has stronger gravity.
   • Io has no oxygen.

6. Wendy jumped 5 feet high. Could she jump that high on Earth? _____

7. Tell about the size of Wendy's room. _____

   _____

8. Name 2 things that were in the room. _____

9. There were maps and lots of other things at the space station to teach people about Jupiter. Name 2 other things. _____

   _____

10. How big is Jupiter compared to the other planets in the solar system?

   • bigger   • smaller   • the same size

11. How long does it take Jupiter to spin around one time?

   _____

12. What place on Io did Wendy and Sidney want to visit?

   _____

13. How far from the space station was the volcano?

   • 30 miles   • half a mile   • 100 meters

B REVIEW ITEMS

1. What planet is shown?

   _____

2. Which is bigger, the "eye" of the planet or Earth?

   _____

GO TO PART D IN YOUR TEXTBOOK

A STORY ITEMS

1. What was the temperature outside the space station?

_____

2. Did it feel cold to Wendy? _____

3. Tell why. _____

_____

4. Wendy and Sidney were running and leaping when they first left the space station. The automatic radio told Wendy if she kept doing what she was doing, she would run out of oxygen in ▭ .

    • 5 minutes   • 35 minutes   • 25 minutes

5. Which uses up more oxygen, **walking** or **running?** _____

6. The girls were heading toward the volcano. What marked the path?

_____

7. What's another name for hot melted rock? _____

8. What name did the volcano have? _____

9. What color is lava when it's very hot? _____

10. What color is lava after it cools a little bit? _____

11. What color is lava after it's completely cooled? _____

12. The inside of the volcano was larger than a _____ .

13. As the girls started to walk around the rim of the volcano, the voice came over Wendy's radio again. How long would Wendy's oxygen last if she kept using it as fast as she had been using it?

    • 45 minutes   • 35 minutes   • 25 minutes

14. What did the girls walk onto to look down into the volcano?

  • a sidewalk   • an overhang   • a slide

15. What happened while they were standing on it?

_____

16. What did Wendy grab? _____

17. What happened to Sidney? _____

_____

1. Which planet in the picture has more gravity? _____

2. How do you know? _____

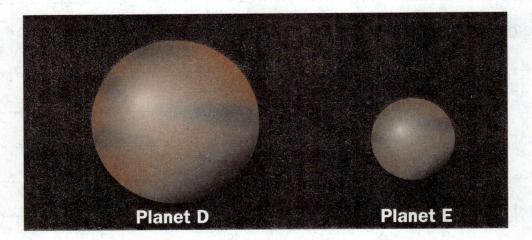

Planet D   Planet E

GO TO PART C IN YOUR TEXTBOOK

A   STORY ITEMS

1. After the overhang fell, Wendy pulled herself up onto the rim of the volcano. Was this **hard** or **easy?** _____

2. Tell why.
   - The gravity was weak.
   - There wasn't any oxygen.
   - She was in a spacesuit.

3. Was Sidney in the lava? _____

4. How close were Sidney's feet to the lava?

   _____

5. Where did Wendy try to go to get help for Sidney?

   _____

6. On the way to get help, the automatic voice came over Wendy's radio. Why?
   - She was using up oxygen too fast.
   - She was not running fast enough.
   - Her spacesuit was getting too hot.

7. Whose voice came over Wendy's radio next? _____

8. What did he tell her to do? _____

9. Wendy ran out of oxygen. Circle **3** things that happened to Wendy.
   - Her arms became stiff.   • Her voice was loud.
   - Her arms became tingly.   • She saw Rod.
   - Her voice wouldn't work.   • She saw spots.

10. About how far from the space station was Wendy when she passed out?
    - 200 centimeters   • 10 yards   • 200 meters

11. Where was Wendy when she woke up? _____

12. How many people were in the vehicle with Wendy? _____

13. Who was driving? _____

14. What did the woman attach to Wendy's spacesuit?

_____

15. Where did the vehicle stop? _____

B **REVIEW ITEMS**

Here's the rule about this electric eye. **Each time the beam of light is broken, the light changes.**

1. The light is off. The beam is broken 4 times. Shade the bulbs that are off.

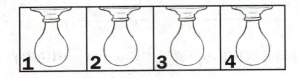

2. Is the light **on** or **off** at the end? _____

3. The light is off. The beam is broken 3 times. Shade the bulbs that are off.

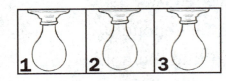

4. Is the light **on** or **off** at the end? _____

5. The light is off. The beam is broken 6 times. Shade the bulbs that are off.

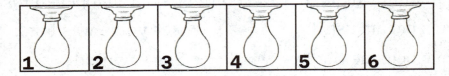

6. Is the light **on** or **off** at the end? _____

GO TO PART C IN YOUR TEXTBOOK

A STORY ITEMS

1. What was Sidney hanging on to when Wendy left for help?

   _____

2. Where was Sidney when Wendy came back?

   _____

3. What did Wendy think had happened to Sidney?

   _____

4. What happened to the end of the rope that fell into the lava?

   _____

5. Who slid down the rope? _____

6. What did he tell Sidney to do?

   _____

7. When Sidney reached the top of the rim, how did she look?
   - healthy   - pale   - sad

8. Why could everybody take their helmets off inside the space station?

   _____

9. Circle **2** words that tell how Sidney felt at the end of the chapter.
   - thirsty   - tired   - cold   - glad

B REVIEW ITEMS

1. How many moons does Jupiter have? _____

2. What planet has more moons, Saturn or Jupiter? _____

3. How much oxygen surrounds Io? _____

4. Does Io move around Jupiter **fast** or **slowly**? _____

5. It takes Io about _____ to go all the way around Jupiter.

6. Which planet in the picture has more gravity? _____

7. How do you know? _____

Planet G   **Planet H**

8. How many Great Lakes are there? _____

9. Color the Great Lakes on the map.

GO TO PART C IN YOUR TEXTBOOK

A   STORY ITEMS

1. How long did the students stay on Io? _____

2. Name 3 things Wendy did after her adventure at Soup Pot.

    1 _____

    2 _____

    3 _____

3. When it was time to go back home to Earth, Wendy felt both happy and
    sad. She felt happy because she would see _____ .

4. She felt sad because she would have to say goodbye to

    _____ .

5. Wendy took lots of pictures of the things she saw. Which pictures did
    Wendy want more than all the rest?

    _____

6. How far away were the big volcanos the girls visited?

    • 200 miles   • 100 miles   • 1 mile

7. Name 2 ways these volcanos were different from Soup Pot.

    1 _____

    2 _____

8. Name 2 things Wendy planned to do when she got back to her hometown.

    1 _____

    2 _____

9. What time of day was it when Traveler Four landed in Japan?

_____

10. Did Wendy and Sidney get on the same plane? _____

11. The woman sitting next to Wendy on the plane was reading a book. What was it about? _____

12. The woman asked about a place that made Wendy laugh. What place was that?
   • Jupiter   • Io   • Saturn

B **REVIEW ITEMS**

1. Write the letter of the footprint made by the heaviest animal. _____

2. Write the letter of the footprint made by the lightest animal. _____

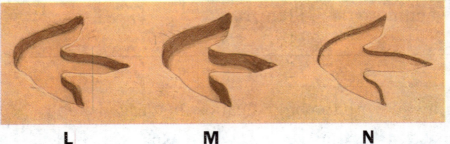

L   M   N

GO TO PART C IN YOUR TEXTBOOK

A   INFORMATION ITEMS

Here are animal names. Label each animal in the picture below.

bear	giraffe	lion	sheep
cow	goat	parrot	squirrel
eagle	hamster	pigeon	tiger
elephant	horse	rabbit	zebra

1. _____

2. _____

3. _____

4. _____

5. _____

6. _____

7. _____

8. _____

9. _____

10. _____

11. _____

12.   Make an **X** on the elephant's trunk.

1. How old was Waldo when he started cooking? _____

2. Did people like Waldo's cooking? _____

3. Who liked Waldo's cooking? _____

4. When the circus animals gathered in Waldo's yard, the weather

   was _____ and the windows were _____ .

5. How did Waldo's family feel about having so many animals in the yard?

   _____

6. What did Waldo use to get the animals back into the truck?

   _____

7. Which animals did Waldo feed in the truck—the circus animals or the

   other animals? _____

8. What did Waldo do after the other animals followed him out of the truck?

   _____

9. Did the animals need to eat a lot of Waldo's food to make them happy?

   _____

10. When the trainers saw Waldo work with the animals, they were .

    • angry   • amazed   • tired

C REVIEW ITEM

Draw arrows at **X**, at **Y**, and at **Z** to show
the way the melted rock moves.

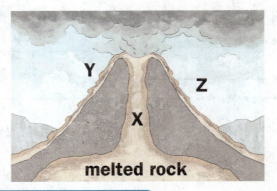

melted rock

GO TO PART D IN YOUR TEXTBOOK

A STORY ITEMS

1. Why did people stay in Waldo's yard after the circus animals left?

    _____

    _____

2. Why couldn't those people see Waldo's legs? _____

    _____

3. How did those people **feel** about the show the animals were putting on?

    _____

4. Why did people from all over make phone calls to Waldo's house?

    _____

5. Waldo's sister thought it was ridiculous when somebody asked her if she'd seen a striped cat. Why did she think it was ridiculous? _____

    _____

6. Waldo came up with a solution to solve a problem with his cooking. What was his solution? _____

7. Did his parents agree with his solution? _____

8. What decision did Waldo's parents make?

    _____

1. Write **north**, **south**, **east**, and **west** in the correct boxes.

2. In which direction is ocean current R moving? _____

3. In which direction is ocean current S moving? _____

4. Which direction is the wind coming from? _____

5. Make an arrow above ice chunk T to show the direction the current will move the ice chunk.

6. Make an arrow next to ice chunk U to show the direction the current will move the ice chunk.

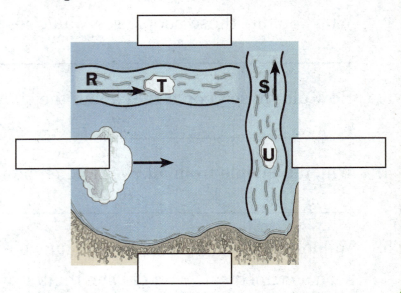

7. Write the missing seasons on the picture below.

8. Shade half of earth J and half of earth L.

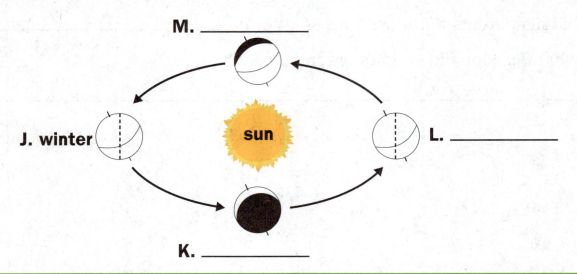

M. _____

J. winter

sun

L. _____

K. _____

GO TO PART C IN YOUR TEXTBOOK

A   INFORMATION ITEMS

1. When you're training an animal, what do you do each time the animal does the trick? _____

2. What do you do if the animal does not do the trick?

    _____

3. Name 2 things you could give to a dog to reward it.

    1 _____

    2 _____

B   STORY ITEMS

1. Waldo's plan had two parts. First, Waldo was going to get _____ .

2. Then he was going to fix up the _____ .

3. What was the first job that Waldo got?

    _____

4. Why didn't he like that job?

    _____

5. What was the second job that Waldo got?

    _____

6. Why didn't he like that job?

    _____

7. What will Waldo do to make the animals in the pet shop happy?

    _____

8. While Waldo was cooking, the pet shop owner opened a window. Why did she do that?

_____

9. Why did Waldo tell her to close the window?

_____

1. Shade the part of the earth where it is nighttime.

2. Which side of the earth is closer to the sun, **J** or **F**? _____

3. Which side of the earth is in nighttime? _____

4. Which side of the earth is in daytime? _____

GO TO PART D IN YOUR TEXTBOOK

A STORY ITEMS

1. What did Mr. Benton want to build at the beginning of the story?

   _____

2. When he was looking at the place where the work would begin, something happened. What was that?

   _____

3. Where did they take Mr. Benton? _____

4. That night he had a dream. Why didn't his clothes fit the way they should?

   _____

5. Who told him in the dream that he should help poor people have pride?

   _____

6. Who told him at the beginning of the story that the new building is not as important as people? _____

7. What did he see going behind a bush at the end of his dream?

   _____

8. What was the name of the fund that fixed up the poor neighborhood?

   _____

9. What is the secret meaning of Tibbar?

   _____

10. Did Tim Benton put people first? _____

11. A message of this story is ▧▧▧ .

    • Rabbits are more important than buildings.

    • People are more important than buildings.

    • Buildings are more important than rabbits.

1. What is the main setting for this story?

   _____

2. Name the main character in this story.

   _____

3. Complete the plot for this story.

   Mr. _____ wanted to tear down homes and build

   an office _____ . He had a _____

   attack and went to the _____ . He dreamed a

   _____ told him to help the neighborhood people.

   With his _____ Fund he helped them. Tibbar is

   _____ spelled backward.

C BACKWARD WORDS

1. <u>Tibbar</u> backward is _____ .

2. <u>Racecar</u> backward is _____ .

3. <u>Evil</u> backward is _____ .

4. The name _____ backward is

   _____ .

A INFORMATION ITEMS

1. When you teach an animal a simple trick, when do you reward the animal?

    _____

2. When don't you reward the animal?

    _____

3. Let's say that you want to teach an animal a very hard trick. Can the animal do the trick at first? _____

4. What will happen if the animal doesn't receive any rewards until it does the trick? _____

5. When you're teaching the animal a hard trick, what do you reward the animal for doing? _____

Let's say you're training a dog to jump up in the air and do a backward somersault. **Use the words below to finish each sentence.**

  • jumping up and turning upside down
  • jumping up in the air
  • jumping up and leaning backward

6. At first you would reward the dog for _____

    _____ .

7. Later you would reward the dog for _____

    _____ .

8. Later you would reward the dog for _____

    _____ .

B STORY ITEMS

1. What's the name of the pet shop owner? _____

2. Why wasn't the pet shop making money? _____

   _____

3. When Waldo let the cats out of their cages, what did Maria think the cats
   would do? _____

4. Did the cats do that? _____

5. What are 2 things the cats did do? _____

   _____

6. After Waldo let all the animals out of their cages, where did he sit down?

   _____

7. Which animals did he feed first? _____

8. What was happening outside of the pet shop window?

   _____

GO TO PART D IN YOUR TEXTBOOK

A STORY ITEMS

1. How many pets did Maria usually sell in a week? _____

2. How many did she sell on the day that Waldo cooked? _____

3. Why did she sell so many more pets when Waldo cooked?

   _____

4. Maria said that she would give Waldo some money for every dollar she makes by selling pets. How much money? _____

5. How did Waldo feel about that deal? _____

6. When Waldo got home, he was out of breath. Tell one reason why.

   _____

7. Why was he late? _____

   _____

8. Waldo changed his plans about cooking in the garage. Where will he cook?

   _____

9. Did his parents like that idea? _____

10. Did Waldo know a lot about training animals? _____

11. How will he learn about training animals?

    _____

12. What will he use as a reward when he trains animals?

    _____

1. In which direction do geese migrate in the fall? _____

2. In which direction do geese migrate in the spring? _____

3. Write the directions **north, south, east,** and **west** in the boxes.

4. Make a line that starts at the circle on the map and goes north.

5. If you start at the circle and move to the number 4, in which direction

   do you go? _____

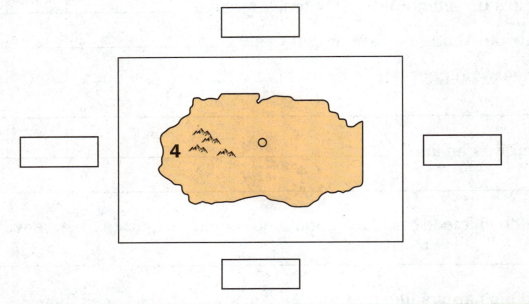

6. **Fill in the blanks to show the four seasons.**

   winter, _____ , summer, fall, _____

   spring, _____ , _____

GO TO PART C IN YOUR TEXTBOOK

A INFORMATION ITEMS

1. Where did Waldo get books about training animals? _____

2. What kind of animals are the easiest to teach? _____

3. What did Waldo train three pigeons to do? _____

4. How long did it take the first pigeon to learn that trick? _____

5. Did it take **more time** or **less time** to train the second pigeon?

   _____

6. What did Waldo attach to the pigeons' feet? _____

7. Why did he do that? _____

8. Where did Waldo put the pigeons after he finished training them?

   _____

9. Why did he do that? _____

10. Maria didn't sell the first three pigeons that Waldo trained. Why not?

    _____

11. How many dancing pigeons did people order the first day? _____

12. Waldo trained a rabbit to walk on a tightrope. Where did he put the ropes
    at first? _____

13. What kind of ropes were they? _____

14. When Waldo put the ropes a few centimeters above the table, he did
    something so the rabbit wouldn't fall. What did he do? _____

    _____

15. What did Waldo do to make a super trick? _____

    _____

1.   How many Great Lakes are there? _____

2.   Color the Great Lakes on the map.

Here's the rule about an electric eye: **Each time the beam of light is broken, the light changes.**

3.   The light is off. The beam is broken 5 times.

Is the light **on** or **off** at the end? _____

4.   The light is off. The beam is broken 7 times.

Is the light **on** or **off** at the end? _____

5.   The light is off. The beam is broken 2 times.

Is the light **on** or **off** at the end? _____

GO TO PART C IN YOUR TEXTBOOK

Name ______________________________

A STORY ITEMS

1. Where will the animal show take place? ______________
2. On what day of the week will it be held? ______________
3. At what time will it start? ______________
4. How much is the admission? ______________
5. Name **3** acts that will be in the animal show.

____

____

____

6. The more water the glass has, the ▬ the sound it makes.
   - higher
   - lower

7. **Cross out** the glass that will make the **highest** ring.
8. **Circle** the glass that will make the **lowest** ring.

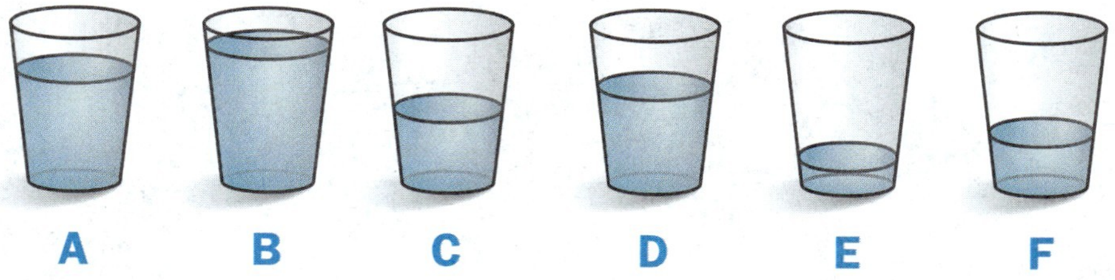

9. What object did the dog use to tap the glasses? ______________
10. What did the dog do with that object at the end of the trick?

____

11. What trick would Gormer the rabbit do? ______________
12. What trick would Henry the cat do? ______________
13. What song did Homer the dog play? ______________

14. Waldo and Maria decided to cook the food for the show at the high school. Why didn't they want to cook it at the pet shop? _____

_____

15. Why wasn't Waldo able to cook his food at the high school?

_____

16. What food will they use for rewards? _____

B   REVIEW ITEM

Draw arrows at **D,** at **E,** and at **F** to show the way the melted rock moves.

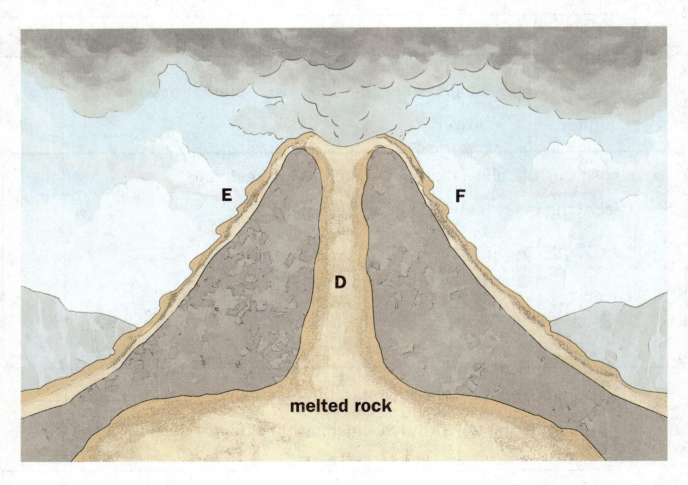

melted rock

GO TO PART C IN YOUR TEXTBOOK

A SKILL ITEMS

east	liquid
north	rocket
muff	walrus
Mercury	earth
admission	
Venus	
funnel	
thousand	
museum	
manufacturers	
attorney	
million	
inventors	
hundred	
off	

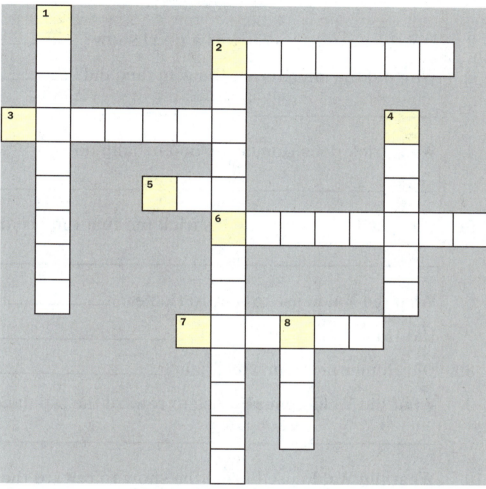

ACROSS

2. A planet that is close to the sun is ▨▨▨ .

3. A word for a **thousand thousands** is a ▨▨▨ .

5. If something is not turned **on,** it is turned ▨▨▨ .

6. Another word for **lawyer** is ▨▨▨ .

7. A place that has many different kinds of exhibits is called a ▨▨▨ .

DOWN

1. The amount you pay to get into a show is called the ▨▨▨ .

2. Inventors usually try to find ▨▨▨ to make their products.

4. A whirlpool is shaped like a ▨▨▨ .

8. **West** is the opposite direction of ▨▨▨ .

1. About how many people came to see the animal show?

   _____

2. Did the people think it was a good show? _____

3. Why did the animals act the way they did? _____

   _____

4. What trick does Homer the dog usually do?

   _____

5. How well did Homer do his trick the first time he did it in the show?

   _____

6. What did Waldo use to reward Homer? _____

7. Did Homer like that reward? _____

8. Did Homer perform well again? _____

9. What did Waldo **usually** use to reward the tap-dancing pigeons?

   _____

10. What did Waldo use during the show to reward the pigeons?

    _____

11. Did the pigeons keep doing their trick for that reward? _____

GO TO PART C IN YOUR TEXTBOOK

A SKILL ITEMS

overboard	ordinary
Alaska	usual
Florida	parent
stomach	restless
normal	city
snow	state
Canada	country
oxygen	blister
sore	

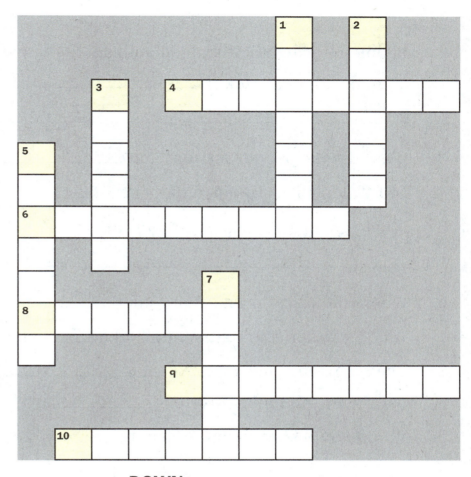

ACROSS

4. Things you see all the time in different places are ▬▬▬▬ things.

6. When things go over the side of a ship, they go ▬▬▬▬ .

8. Geese that are black, brown, and white are called ▬▬▬▬ geese.

9. When you feel ▬▬▬▬ , you don't want to keep doing what you're doing.

10. Japan is a ▬▬▬▬ .

DOWN

1. You may get a ▬▬▬▬ on your foot if your shoe doesn't fit well.

2. Oomoo and Oolak lived in the state of ▬▬▬▬ .

3. When Wendy was on Io, she had to wear an ▬▬▬▬ tank so she could breathe.

5. If you are hungry, your ▬▬▬▬ may make noise.

7. Your mother is called your ▬▬▬▬ .

1. How did the people in the audience feel about the animal show?

   _____

2. People returned their trained animals to the pet shop. Why wouldn't those animals do their tricks? _____

   _____

3. What did the people ask for? _____

4. Did Waldo eat very much dinner? _____

5. What was he thinking about during dinner?

   _____

6. Where did he go right after dinner? _____

7. Waldo's father said that Waldo had a _____ problem.

8. The animals would work for _____ , but they would not work for _____ .

9. Waldo could solve this problem by training the animals to work for

   _____ .

GO TO PART C IN YOUR TEXTBOOK

A SKILL ITEMS

flocks · disturb
Saturn · hitch
tune
reward
herds
incredible
green
audience
brown
Mercury
chant
experience
terrific
Jupiter

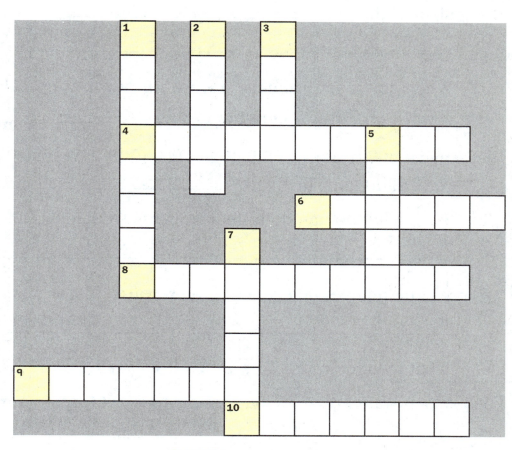

ACROSS

4. Another word for **amazing** is ▅▅▅▅ .

6. Geese live in large groups called ▅▅▅▅ .

8. Each thing you do is an ▅▅▅▅ .

9. Io is a moon of the planet ▅▅▅▅ .

10. Another word for **bother** is ▅▅▅▅ .

DOWN

1. The people who watch an event are called the ▅▅▅▅ .

2. Here's another way of saying **He will tie the dog to the sled: He will ▅▅▅▅ the dog to the sled.**

3. Another word for a **song** is a ▅▅▅▅ .

5. Jupiter is orange, white, and ▅▅▅▅ .

7. Something you get for doing a good job is a ▅▅▅▅ for doing that job.

1. Waldo read until late at night and then went to bed. Why didn't he go to sleep right away? _____

   _____

2. When you teach animals to work for new rewards, do you change the reward **quickly** or **slowly?** _____

3. When you teach an animal to work for a new reward, what kind of reward do you start with? _____

4. Then what do you do to that reward? _____

   _____

5. When do you stop changing the reward? _____

   _____

6. What reward do Waldo's animals work for? _____

7. When Waldo teaches his animals to work for new rewards, what reward will he start with? _____

8. Then what will he do to that reward?

   _____

9. How long did the school day seem to Waldo? _____

10. Where did he go right after school? _____

11. What did he start doing as soon as he got there?

    _____

GO TO PART C IN YOUR TEXTBOOK

A STORY ITEMS

Fill in each blank with the word **regular** or the word **coated.**

1. Waldo trained the pigeons to work for a new reward. First, Waldo rewarded the pigeons with his special food. Next, Waldo rewarded the pigeons with two _____ seeds.

2. Next, Waldo rewarded the pigeons with two _____ seeds and one _____ seed.

3. Next, Waldo rewarded the pigeons with two _____ seeds and one _____ seed.

4. At the end, Waldo rewarded the pigeons with three _____ seeds.

5. Waldo trained the rabbit to work for a new reward. First, Waldo rewarded the rabbit with his special food. Next, Waldo rewarded the rabbit with two pieces of _____ carrots.

6. Next, Waldo rewarded the rabbit with two pieces of _____ carrots and one piece of _____ carrot.

7. At the end, Waldo rewarded the rabbit with three pieces of _____ carrots.

Fill in each blank with the word **top** or the word **bottom.**

8. A **regular pyramid** has one animal at the _____ of the pyramid.

9. An **upside-down pyramid** has one animal at the _____ of the pyramid.

truck
kayak
pole
boring
crater
Canada
Alaska
volcano
instant
drifting
equator
clever
hotter
ignore
colder
earthquake
automobile

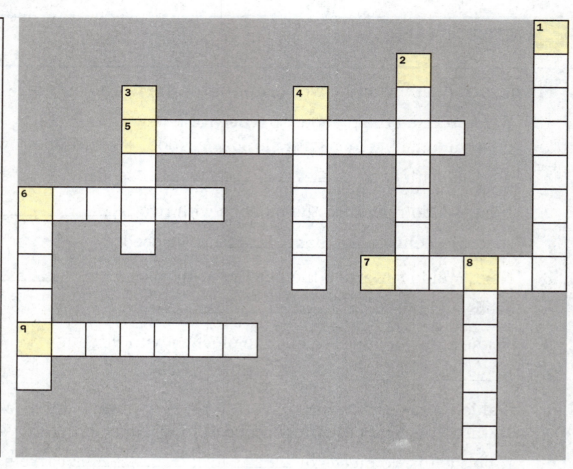

ACROSS

5. Another word for **car** is ▮▮▮▮ .

6. Most wild geese are born in ▮▮▮▮ .

7. **Interesting** is the opposite of ▮▮▮▮ .

9. The part of Earth that receives more heat than any other part is the ▮▮▮▮ .

DOWN

1. When an ice chunk is being moved by a current, we say that the ice chunk is ▮▮▮▮ .

2. A mountain that erupts is called a ▮▮▮▮ .

3. The kind of boat that Inuits use is a ▮▮▮▮ .

4. The farther you go from the equator, the ▮▮▮▮ you get.

6. Another word for **very smart** is ▮▮▮▮ .

8. When you don't pay attention to something, you ▮▮▮▮ that thing.

GO TO PART C IN YOUR TEXTBOOK

A   INFORMATION ITEMS

1. In what country are the states of Colorado and Utah?

    _____

2. Name the mountains you drive over to get from Colorado to Utah.

    _____

3. In which direction do you go to get from Colorado to Utah? _____

4. Name 2 cities in Colorado you read about today.

    _____

5. Name the city in Utah you read about today. _____

6. Write **north, south, east,** and **west** in the correct boxes.

7. Make an **R** on the state of Colorado.

8. Make a **T** on the state of Utah.

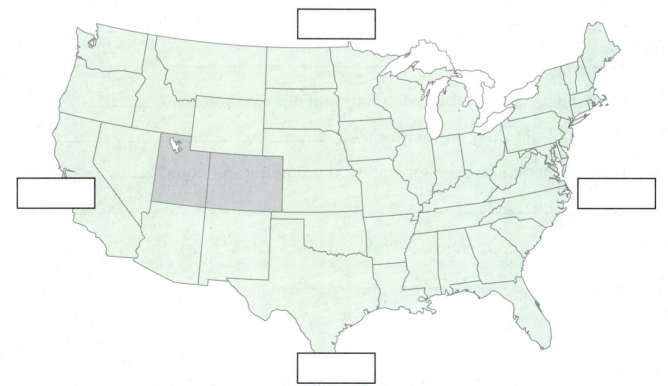

1. What animal was at the bottom of the upside-down pyramid?

   _____

2. Which dog stood on the huge dog's rear end?

   _____

3. Which dog stood with its paws on the huge dog's head?

   _____

4. How many cats were in the pyramid? _____

5. What animals did the cats stand on? _____

6. How many rabbits were in the pyramid? _____

7. What animals did the rabbits stand on? _____

8. How many pigeons were in the pyramid? _____

9. What animals did the pigeons stand on? _____

10. Waldo and Maria didn't show the upside-down pyramid before the animal

    show. Why not? _____

    _____

11. How many times did the dancing pigeons do their act? _____

12. How well did they do their act? _____

13. How did the audience respond to the dancing pigeons? _____

    _____

14. What did the audience do while Homer played "Mary Had a Little Lamb"?

    _____

GO TO PART D IN YOUR TEXTBOOK

A POEM ITEMS

1. Each part of a poem is called a ▇▇▇ .

   • story   • stanza   • chapter

2. The author says this pancake collection is <u>unique</u>. What does <u>unique</u> mean?

   • There are many like it.

   • There are none like it.

3. Circle each place where the author keeps pancakes.

   • in closets   • in the freezer

   • in boxes   • in the bureaus

   • in the backyard   • on carpets

   • in the car   • in pockets

   • on shelves   • on hangers

4. At the end of the poem, the author plans to make more pancakes. How many more?

   • dozens   • twenty   • hundreds

5. **The stanzas build on each other. Match each stanza to its description.**

   Stanza 1 tells us •   • to go home.

   Stanza 2 tells us •   • more about how the pancakes look.

   Stanza 5 tells us •   • the pancakes are unique.

   Stanza 7 tells us •   • more about where the pancakes are.

WRITING ABOUT A COLLECTION

Write about a collection you would like to have most. Tell about some of the things that would be in that collection. Tell why you would really like to have the collection and what you would do with the things in the collection. You may also draw a picture of the collection you'd like to have.

_____

_____

_____

_____

_____

_____

_____

END OF LESSON 80

A STORY ITEMS

1. When the animals did the super trick at Samson High School, what did the birds do before they landed on the rabbits?

   _____

2. How did Waldo signal the birds to land on the rabbits?

   _____

3. How did the audience feel about the pyramid act?

   _____

4. Some people put in special orders for trained animals. Name one of those special orders. _____

5. What time of year is usually the busiest for the pet shop? _____

6. Did the pet shop have **more business** or **less business** than it had at Christmas? _____

7. What's a tour? _____

8. How long would Waldo's tour last? _____

9. How many shows is Maria planning for the tour? _____

10. How will Waldo keep up with his schoolwork while he's on the tour?

    _____

11. What will Waldo and Maria ride in when they travel from city to city?

    _____

12. What will the animals travel in? _____

13. Who will drive? _____

14. Before Waldo could go, he would need _____ from his parents.

involve	lower	Triceratops	gravity	tire	shortly
Rocky	higher	Tyrannosaurus	selected	regular	waste
contacted	clever	information	hire	deserve	

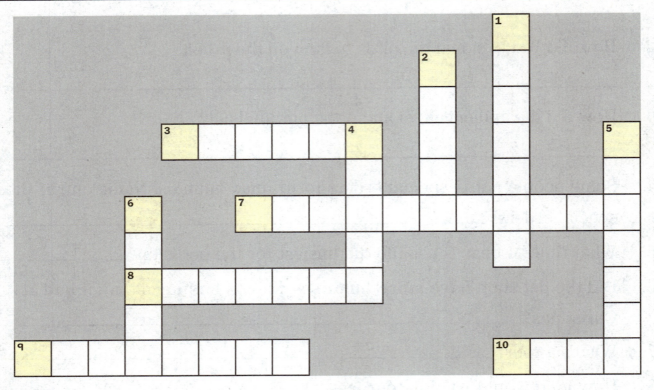

ACROSS

3. Another word for **very smart** is ▬▬▬ .

7. The name of the dinosaur that had horns and armor was ▬▬▬ .

8. Another word for **soon** is ▬▬▬ .

9. Another word for **chose** is ▬▬▬ .

10. When you give someone a job, you ▬▬▬ that person.

DOWN

1. Bigger planets have more ▬▬▬ than smaller planets.

2. The more water the glass has, the ▬▬▬ the sound it makes.

4. To get from Colorado to Utah, you cross the ▬▬▬ Mountains.

5. Something you should receive is something you ▬▬▬ .

6. When we use something the wrong way, we ▬▬▬ that thing.

GO TO PART C IN YOUR TEXTBOOK

A   STORY ITEMS

1. Who did Waldo's father want to talk to before he gave Waldo permission to go on the tour? _____

2. What did Waldo's father think after he talked to Maria?

    _____

3. How many shows did Waldo and Maria do **before** they got to Denver? ____

4. Which city did Waldo and Maria go to **after** Denver? _____

5. Which brakes stopped working first—the truck brakes or the trailer brakes?

    _____

6. Where was the truck when the brakes failed? _____

- Write **B** in front of each thing that happened **before** the tour.
- Write **D** in front of each thing that happened **during** the tour.

7. _____ The driver hooked up the line for the trailer brakes.

8. _____ Waldo saw a mountain goat.

9. _____ Waldo's parents gave permission for Waldo to go on the trip.

10. _____ The driver explained why the trailer needed brakes.

11. _____ Maria and Waldo stopped studying and looked at the mountains.

12. _____ Waldo and Maria did a show in Denver, Colorado.

13. _____ Waldo and Maria did a show at Samson High School.

14. How did the truck engine sound to Waldo at the end of the chapter?

    _____

15. What did Waldo smell at the end of the chapter? _____

Look at the picture.

1. Shade the part of Earth where it is nighttime.

2. Which side of Earth is closer to the sun, **J** or **K?** _____

3. Which side of Earth is in nighttime? _____

4. Which side of Earth is in daytime? _____

5. Write **north, south, east,** and **west** in the correct boxes.

6. In which direction is ocean current L moving? _____

7. In which direction is ocean current M moving? _____

8. Which direction is the wind coming from?

   _____

9. Make an arrow above ice chunk N to show the direction the current will move the ice chunk.

10. Make an arrow above ice chunk P to show the direction the current will move the ice chunk.

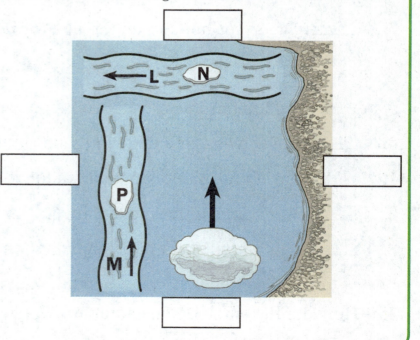

GO TO PART C IN YOUR TEXTBOOK

A STORY ITEMS

1. Why couldn't the driver stop the truck? _____

   _____

2. How many pounds of weight do you have to push down with to make the emergency brake work? _____

3. If the huge dog had **all** its weight on the brake, would the brake work? _____

4. Did the huge dog weigh **more than 100 pounds** or **less than 100 pounds?**

   _____

5. How many paws did the huge dog have on the brake? _____

6. Was the weight of the three dogs enough to slow down the trailer?

   _____

7. Was that enough to make the brake stop the trailer very fast? _____

8. Why was it important for the trailer to stop fast? _____

   _____

9. What did Waldo do to get more weight on the brake? _____

   _____

B REVIEW ITEMS

1. Write the names of the 8 planets, starting with the planet closest to the sun.

   _____

2. In which direction do geese migrate in the fall? _____

3. In which direction do geese migrate in the spring? _____

4. Write the directions **north, south, east,** and **west** in the boxes.

5. Make a line that starts at the circle on the map and goes north.

6. If you start at the circle and move to the number 5, in which direction do you go? _____

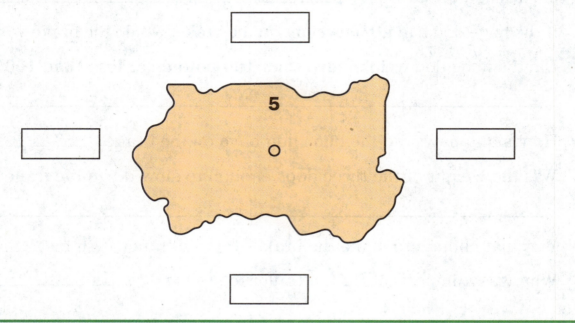

7. How many moons does Jupiter have? _____

8. How many moons does Saturn have? _____

9. Which planet has more moons, Saturn or Jupiter? _____

10. How far is it from Earth to Jupiter? _____

11. Do gases surround Io? _____

12. How much oxygen is on Io? _____

GO TO PART C IN YOUR TEXTBOOK

A **INFORMATION ITEMS**

Write the name of each kind of coral below the picture.

- **red coral**
- **staghorn coral**
- **brain coral**

1. _____   2. _____   3. _____

4. Coral is made up of the _____ of tiny

_____ .

5. An underwater hill that is covered with coral is called a coral _____ .

6. Where do the animals that make up a coral reef spend their whole life?

- all over the ocean
- in one place

B **STORY ITEMS**

1. The weight of three dogs and four cats was on the emergency brake. Was that more than 80 pounds? _____

2. Was that enough weight to stop the truck? _____

3. To keep the brake locked in place, the driver turned _____ .

4. After the truck had stopped, what treat did Waldo give the animals?

   _____ .

5. Why did he give them a treat? _____

   _____

6. What trick did the animals do for the people who gathered around the

   truck? _____

7. How long did it take to get the brakes fixed? _____

8. Where did the truck and trailer go after the brakes were fixed?

   _____

9. What followed the truck and trailer? _____

10. Waldo remembered one show as the greatest show his animals ever did.

    Where did that show take place? _____

    _____

C   SKILL ITEMS

Here are 3 events that happened in the chapter. Write **beginning, middle,**
or **end** for each event.

1. The show in Utah was a great success. _____

2. The truck was at the curve now, but it was hardly moving.

   _____

3. Two other police officers were directing traffic around the truck
   and trailer.

   _____

GO TO PART D IN YOUR TEXTBOOK

A STORY ITEMS

1. What was Alma deathly afraid of? _____

2. Name 2 things Alma wasn't afraid of. _____

    _____

3. How would Alma feel when water got up to her neck?

    _____

4. Name 2 acts of bravery. _____

    _____

5. Complete the rule about being brave. To be brave, you must do things

    that are _____ .

6. Was holding snakes an act of bravery for Alma? _____

7. Tell why. _____

    _____

8. Was swimming an act of bravery for Alma? _____

9. Tell why. _____

    _____

10. Where was Alma going to take swimming lessons?

    _____

11. What sign did Alma have to show that she became frightened when she

    thought about swimming? _____

1. Write the missing seasons on the picture below.

2. Shade half of Earth R and half of Earth T.

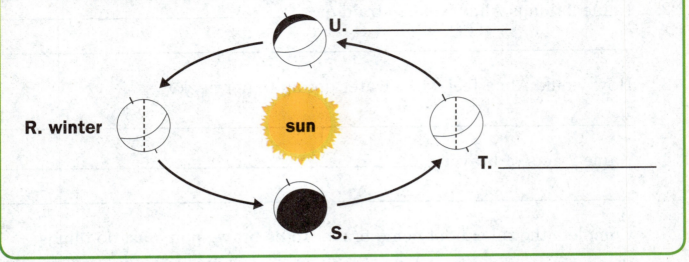

R. winter

U. _____

T. _____

S. _____

3. Which uses more oxygen, running or sitting? _____

4. What's another name for hot, melted rock? _____

GO TO PART C IN YOUR TEXTBOOK

A INFORMATION ITEMS

1. When you dive down 33 feet, you have _____ times the pressure on you that you have at the surface.

2. When you dive down 66 feet, you have _____ times the pressure on you that you have at the surface.

Write the missing numbers in the blanks.

_____0_____ feet	surface pressure
3. _____ feet	2 times surface pressure
4. _____ feet	3 times surface pressure
5. _____ feet	4 times surface pressure

6. Write the letter of the body that has the **least** pressure on it.

    _____

7. Write the letter of the body that has the **most** pressure on it.

    _____

8. Write the letters of all the bodies that have **more** pressure on them than **D** has on it.

    _____

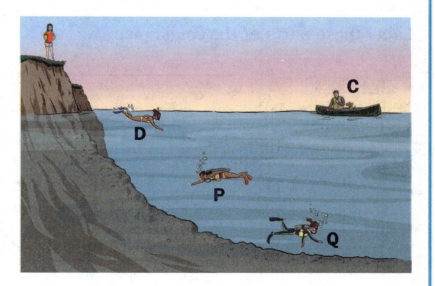

STORY ITEMS

1. What does the color of water tell you about the water?

    _____

2. Name **2** things Alma did when she was learning to swim.

    _____

    _____

3. What was Alma getting ready to do in this chapter? _____

    _____

4. What problem did Alma have with her scuba mask the first time she tried

    to wear it? _____

5. How did she **feel** when that happened? _____

6. What was the deepest dive Alma had ever made? _____

7. How deep will she dive this time? _____

Label these parts of the scuba gear.

- air hose

- mouthpiece

- fins

- mask

- dial

- air tank

- wet suit

8. _____

9. _____

10. _____

11. _____

12. _____

13. _____

14. _____

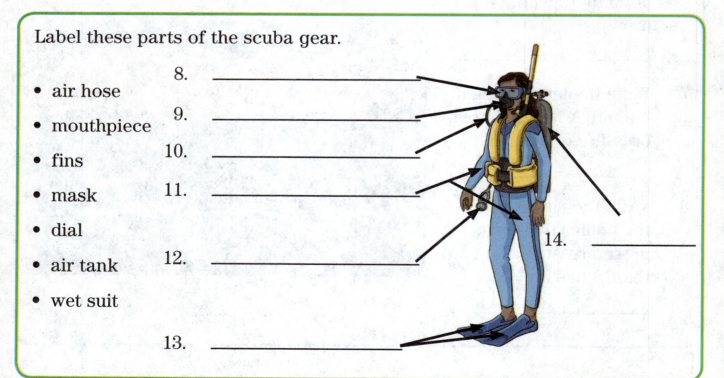

GO TO PART D IN YOUR TEXTBOOK

A STORY ITEMS

1. The diving boat was about _____ miles east of the United States.

2. Name the islands that are near the place they are diving.

   _____

3. Were the divers **north** or **south** of those islands? _____

4. In what ocean are they diving? _____

5. What did the guide tell the divers to do if they got separated?

   _____

6. How deep were the divers at the end of the chapter? _____

7. How deep are the divers going to go? _____

8. If you go underwater that deep, the pressure is much greater than it is on land. How many times greater is it? _____

9. When divers are that deep, how long should they take to return to the surface of the water? _____

10. If the divers go up faster than that they may get bubbles in their

    _____ .

11. What made Alma's ears hurt? _____

12. How deep was she when they started to hurt? _____

13. If you move up too fast from very deep water, you may get the

    _____ .

14. What forms in your blood as you go up too fast? _____

15. When you go up very fast, is there **more pressure** or **less pressure** on your body? _____

Fill in the blanks to show how deep the divers would be.

16. When the diver is _____ feet underwater, the pressure is two times as great as it is on land.

17. When the diver is _____ feet underwater, the pressure is three times as great as it is on land.

18. When the diver is _____ feet underwater, the pressure is four times as great as it is on land.

19. Could Alma feel the weight of her air tank underwater? _____

20. Could Alma feel the pressure of the water? _____

21. Name **2** things that were part of the incredible scene that Alma and Marta saw.

     _____

22. When Alma looked at the other divers below her, what did she think they looked like? _____

23. What happened each time a diver breathed? _____

     _____

24. What did the diving guide point out to the group?

     _____

25. When you open a bottle of soda pop, what happens to the pressure inside the bottle? _____

26. What forms in the soda pop? _____

GO TO PART C IN YOUR TEXTBOOK

A STORY ITEMS

1. How deep did the divers go? _____

2. About how long did it take them to get there? _____

3. Did things look **darker** or **lighter** at the bottom? _____

4. There weren't as many plants down there because there wasn't as much

   _____ .

5. Name **3** things that great water pressure was doing to Alma.

   _____

   _____

   _____

6. Why did the bubbles following the divers look dark gray?

   _____

7. What is the name of the arrow-shaped fish that Alma saw?

   _____

8. Write **2** facts Alma knew about these fish.

   _____

   _____

9. Is the water cooler **at 100 feet down** or **at the surface?**

   _____

10. Is all the water at 100 feet down the same temperature? _____

11. What should a diver's bubbles look like? _____

12. What did Marta's bubbles look like? _____

13. What did that mean? _____

14. Marta started to go to the surface very fast. Why did Alma want to catch Marta? _____

_____

15. Who could swim faster, Alma or Marta? _____

Answer these questions about a buoyancy device:

16. What do you fill the device with? _____

17. When it is filled up, what happens to the diver? _____

_____

18. When it is empty, what happens to the diver? _____

_____

19. What hard decision did Alma have to make after she caught up

with Marta? _____

_____

20. What did Alma decide to do? _____

_____

21. Did Marta give the air hose back to Alma? _____

22. Marta didn't know what she was doing because she was in a state of

_____ .

GO TO PART C IN YOUR TEXTBOOK

A **INFORMATION ITEMS**

1. In what state is the Iditarod sled-dog race? _____

2. In which city does it begin? _____

3. In which city does it end? _____

4. The Iditarod is about ▨▨▨ miles from start to finish.

   - 500   • 1000   • 1600

5. In most years, the race takes about ▨▨▨ .

   - a week   • 9 days   • 2 weeks

6. The person who drives a sled-dog team is called a _____ .

7. The drivers of the sled-dog teams command the dogs by using their ▨▨▨ .

   - ropes   • steering wheels   • voices

B **STORY ITEMS**

1. As Alma and Marta moved up to the surface of the water, they had to stop ten feet below the surface. How long did they wait there?

   _____

2. Why didn't the girls go straight up to the surface? _____

   _____

3. How did the water pressure change as the girls moved toward the surface? _____

   _____

4. How did the light around them change as they moved toward the surface? _____

coral	overcome	Colorado	understand	emergency	instructor
bends	reef	California	surface	buoyant	suffer
oxygen	Utah	bare	success	bubbles	musher

ACROSS

2. Another word for **teacher** is ▉ .

4. When you solve a problem, you ▉ the problem.

6. A brake you use if the regular brake doesn't work is called an ▉ brake.

8. When you open a bottle of soda pop, ▉ form in the pop.

10. One of the states in the western part of the United States is ▉ .

DOWN

1. When you do very well at something, you have ▉ .

3. An underwater hill that's covered with coral is called a coral ▉ .

5. The person who drives a sled-dog team is called a ▉ .

7. ▉ is made up of the skeletons of tiny animals.

9. If divers move up fast from deep water, they may get the ▉ .

GO TO PART D IN YOUR TEXTBOOK

A STORY ITEMS

1. Elena was Yanaba's ▓▓▓▓ .
    - sister   - grandmother   - school friend

2. Circle 3 things that are true about Elena's bracelet.

3. Underline 3 things that are true about Yanaba's hair clip.
    - made of wood   - bought at the mission   - hummingbird
    - Grandmother made it.   - made of silver   - crow

4. Did Yanaba want a silver bracelet like Elena's? _____

5. What did Yanaba think the bracelet would bring her?

    _____

6. Did Yanaba get a silver bracelet like Elena's? _____

7. Why did Yanaba and Grandmother go for a walk together?

    _____

    _____

8. Did Yanaba and Grandmother walk all the way back to the village

    together? _____

9. Did Yanaba have an easy time returning to the village? _____

10. At the end of the day, Grandmother said it had been a very

    _____ day.

11. What do you think is the message of this story?

    _____

END OF LESSON 90

A   INFORMATION ITEMS

1. Most sled-dog teams have an ▮▮▮▮ number of dogs.
   - even   • odd

2. For the Iditarod, a sled-dog team can't have more than
   _____ dogs.

3. Which letter shows the swing dogs? _____

4. Which letter shows the wheel dogs? _____

5. Which letter shows the lead dogs? _____

6. Which letter shows where the musher is most of the time? _____

7. Which letter shows the gangline? _____

8. Which letter shows tug lines? _____

Use these words to answer items 9–11:

- **wheel dogs**   • **lead dogs**   • **swing dogs**

9. The important job of these dogs is to free the sled when it gets stuck.

_____

10. These dogs are very smart, and other dogs obey them. _____

11. These dogs follow very well, and they are fast. _____

B STORY ITEMS

1. What town does Susie live near? _____

2. In what state does she live? _____

3. What's the name of her dog? _____

4. Susie's Uncle Chad was getting ready for _____ .

5. Susie went to Chad's place on a _____ .

6. What kind of sled dog was Susie's dog? _____

7. Was he going to be part of Chad's regular sled-dog team? _____

8. How many times had Chad entered the Iditarod before? _____

9. How many times had he finished the race at Nome? _____

10. What was his goal for the Iditarod this year? _____

11. This year's race would begin in a little more than _____ weeks.

12. Chad drove the dogs and his sled to ▨▨▨ .

- Eagle Claw Valley   • Moose River Valley   • Eagle River Valley

13. Chad wanted to find out what the team would do in really ▨▨▨ .

- cold weather   • rough country   • flat country

GO TO PART D IN YOUR TEXTBOOK

A INFORMATION ITEMS

1. What do sled dogs wear to protect their feet? _____

2. Circle the 2 items that tell what could happen to a sled dog's feet if they don't have protection.

   - snowballs between the pads   - cuts from ice and frozen snow
   - stiff legs   - long claws

3. The booties that Chad likes best are made of _____ .

4. If booties are too tight, what could happen? _____

   _____

5. If booties are too loose, what could happen? _____

   _____

B STORY ITEMS

1. How many dogs did Chad plan to run in the Iditarod? _____

2. How many dogs did Chad start with at Eagle River Valley? _____

3. How many dogs did Susie keep on leashes? _____

4. Why did Chad put bags of dirt on the sled? _____

   _____

5. The dogs wore something they didn't usually wear for practice runs. What was that? _____

6. Why did they wear them for this run? _____

   _____

7. What command tells sled dogs to turn left? _____

8. What command tells them to turn right? _____

9. What command tells them to move straight ahead? _____

10. What did Chad do to test the dogs?

    • He got the sled stuck against rocks.   • He ran the dogs along the road.
              • He did not tell the dogs what to do.

C REVIEW ITEMS

1. Write **north, south, east,** and **west** in the correct boxes.

2. In which direction is ocean current B moving? _____

3. In which direction is ocean current C moving? _____

4. Which direction is the wind coming from? _____

5. Make an arrow above ice chunk D to show the direction the current will move the chunk.

6. Make an arrow above ice chunk E to show the direction the current will move the chunk.

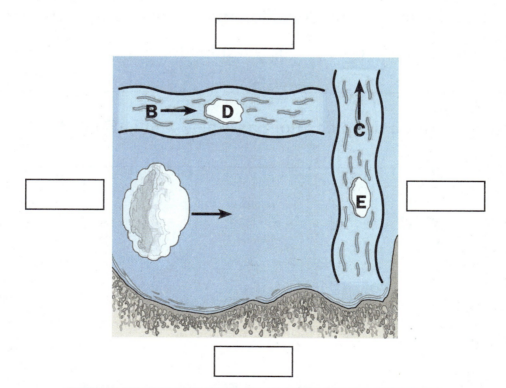

GO TO PART D IN YOUR TEXTBOOK

A INFORMATION ITEMS

1. To get the sled free, Chad first gave commands to the

   _____ dogs.

2. When the sled tipped over, the dogs on leashes thought Chad was ▮▮▮▮ .

   • awkward   • playing   • angry

3. Why didn't some of the dogs on the gangline run over to Chad?

   _____

4. During most of the practice, how many dogs were on the gangline?

   _____

5. At the end of the practice, how many dogs were on the gangline?

   _____

6. Which number of dogs was easier to handle? _____

7. Which number of dogs made a more powerful team? _____

8. When were the dogs going to be examined?

   _____

9. What happens if a dog does not pass the examination?

   _____

avoid	strain	barracuda	booties	shark
leash	gang	left	gee	lead
tug	swing	haw	wheel	mush
purpose	Alaska	Nome	equator	Anchorage

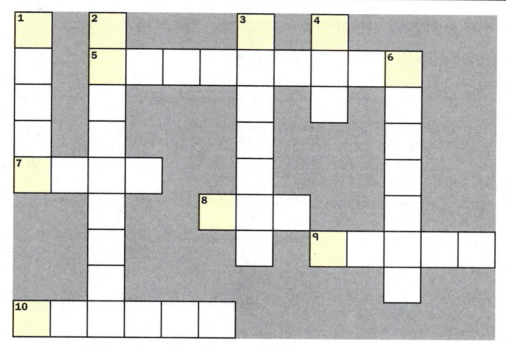

ACROSS

5. The city where the Iditarod begins is ▨▨▨ .

7. The ▨▨▨ dogs on a sled-dog team are very smart, and other dogs obey them.

8. The command that tells sled dogs to turn right is ▨▨▨ .

9. When you stay away from something, you ▨▨▨ that thing.

10. The Iditarod is held in the state of ▨▨▨ . .

DOWN

1. The important job of the ▨▨▨ dogs on a sled-dog team is to free the sled when it gets stuck.

2. An arrow-shaped fish is a ▨▨▨ .

3. Sled dogs wear ▨▨▨ to protect their feet.

4. The command that tells sled dogs to turn left is ▨▨▨ .

6. The make-believe line around the middle of Earth is called the ▨▨▨ .

GO TO PART C IN YOUR TEXTBOOK

Name _____

1. At the beginning of today's chapter, who was late in the morning?

    _____

2. Susie was surprised to see which dog in the truck? _____

3. Chad told Susie that he planned to run _____ dogs.

4. How did that make Susie feel? _____

5. Which 2 dogs would now be on the team?

    _____

6. What does a musher have to do with any dog that is injured during the

    Iditarod? _____

7. What did Chad plan to do with some dogs if he had trouble with a team

    of sixteen? _____

8. According to the rules, there must be at least how many dogs on the

    gangline at the end of the Iditarod? _____

9. The veterinarian found out that one dog had a problem. Which dog?

    _____

10. What was the problem? _____

11. What job does that dog have on Chad's team? _____

Write the missing numbers in the blanks.

___0___ feet	surface pressure
1. _____ feet	2 times surface pressure
2. _____ feet	3 times surface pressure
3. _____ feet	4 times surface pressure

4. Write the missing seasons on the picture below.

5. Shade half of Earth W and half of Earth Y.

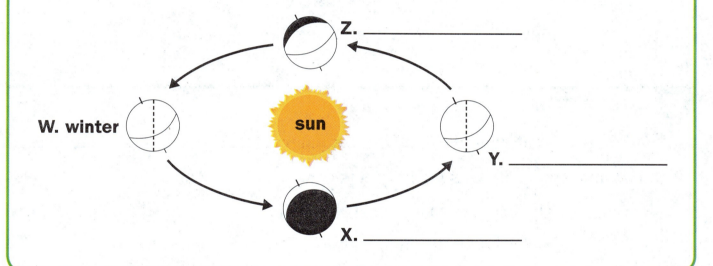

Z. _____

W. winter   sun   Y. _____

X. _____

GO TO PART C IN YOUR TEXTBOOK

A INFORMATION ITEMS

1. The rules for the Iditarod say the musher must have certain things. Circle those things.

    - enough food for a day
    - wood to make a fire
    - an ax
    - enough food for a week
    - another pair of shoes

    - cooker and pot
    - a tent
    - a good sleeping bag
    - snowshoes
    - extra dogs

2. How many extra sets of booties for each dog must the musher pack? _____

3. The sled must have room to hold [____] .

    - another musher
    - an injured dog
    - a spare sled

B STORY ITEMS

1. What did Chad decide to do with Chugger? _____

2. He gave some reasons for his decision. Circle 2 reasons.

    - She had always been the fastest runner.
    - She had never had any hip problems.
    - She was frequently sick.
    - Neither of her parents had hip problems.
    - She was only three years old.

3. What's the name of the woman whose picture was on Susie's wall?

    _____

4. How many times did she enter the Iditarod? _____

5. How many times did she finish in first place? _____

6. On March 15, what was the weather like when the race began?

   _____

7. How many mushers start the race at the same time?

   • 1   • 2   • 10   • all

8. How much time passes before the next musher starts? _____

9. What number was Chad? _____

10. The musher in front of Chad was from _____ .

11. When mushers are on the trail, how much help can they get from

    someone else? _____

C   REVIEW ITEMS

Look at the picture below.

1. Shade the part of Earth where it is nighttime.

2. Which side of Earth is closer to the sun, **W** or **X?** _____

sun

3. Which side of Earth is in nighttime? _____

4. Which side of Earth is in daytime? _____

GO TO PART D IN YOUR TEXTBOOK

A   INFORMATION ITEMS

1.   Why are checkpoints called checkpoints? _____

_____

2.   Name **3** things mushers do at checkpoints.

_____

_____

_____

3.   How does food get to the checkpoints?

_____

4.   Most of the checkpoints are closer than _____ miles apart.

5.   About how many checkpoints are there between Anchorage and Nome?

_____

B   STORY ITEMS

1.   Just before Chad left, Susie became worried. What worried her?

_____

2.   Was Chad **calm** or **nervous?** _____

3.   What was the name of the woman who left just before Chad?

_____

4.   How do mushers get water for their dogs? _____

_____

5.   When there is no straw, mushers sometimes make beds for their dogs with

_____ .

6. When Libby Riddles won the Iditarod in 1985, the weather was ▓▓▓ .
    • very bad   • average   • very good

7. Circle the items that tell what Chad saw or felt when he was 150 miles into the race.
    • frozen lakes   • blasting wind
    • 10 degrees below zero   • flat trail
    • rough country   • mountains
    • hard, icy snow   • warm
    • blowing snow   • sunny
    • soft snow   • 10 degrees above zero

8. What was the name of the pass Chad was getting close to?

    _____

9. Why did he think that name was funny?

    _____

10. What's the name of the first woman to win the Iditarod?

    _____

11. In what year did she win it? _____

12. Where were she and most of the mushers when the race was stopped the first time? _____

13. Why did Susie write a different letter after she heard the TV report?

    _____

14. In the letter she didn't send, what did she write about?

    _____

15. What did the race officials think they would have to do if the bad weather continued? _____

GO TO PART D IN YOUR TEXTBOOK

A STORY ITEMS

1. Would the snow be deeper **on the trail** or **off the trail?**

   _____

2. Why? _____

3. If Chad had stayed on the trail, he would have gone in which direction?

   _____

4. How did he figure out which direction he was going? _____

   _____

5. Did he turn **left** or **right** in order to go in the correct direction? _____

6. When the wind finally died down, how much daylight was there?

   _____

7. What could Chad see? _____

8. How did the dogs know they were near the checkpoint? _____

   _____

9. How did they act? _____

10. When Chad arrived at the lodge, how many mushers were missing? _____

11. What was the name of one of those mushers? _____

12. How did Chad show the officials the route he had taken?

    _____

13. When did Chad see one of the missing mushers?

    _____

B SKILL ITEMS

Esther	Mars	Venus	thorough	veterinarian	examination
vocabulary	Riddles	fierce	doctor	Susan	test
Butcher	Iditarod	sixteen	fifteen	Libby	cruel

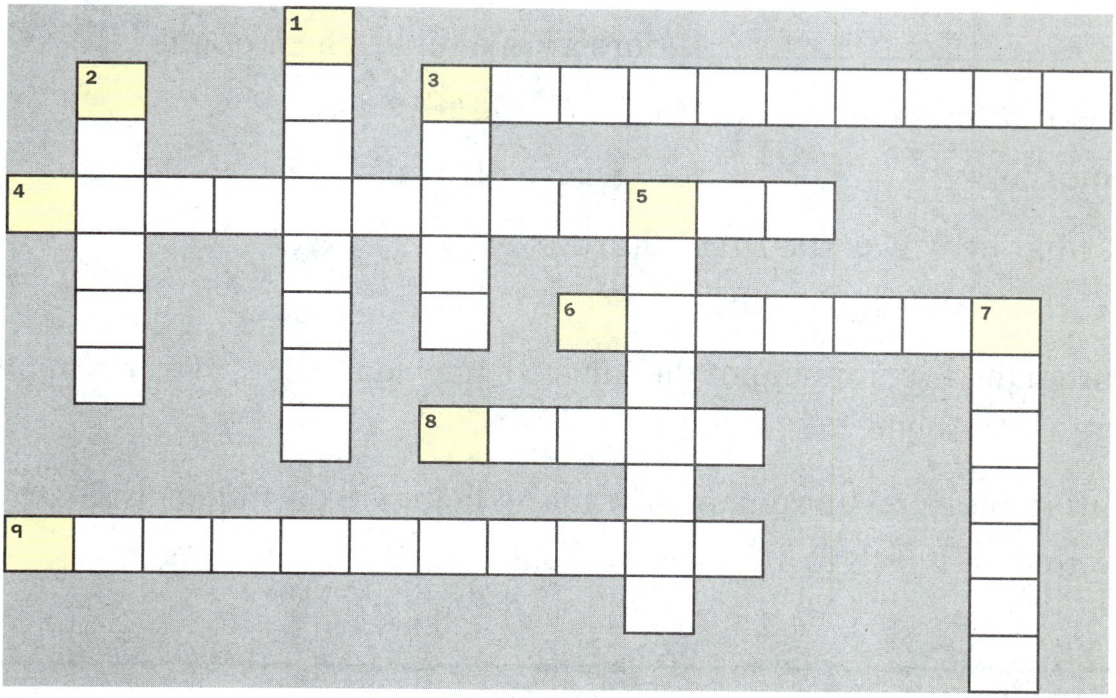

ACROSS

3. All the words a person knows is called the person's ______ .
4. Another word for **animal doctor** is ______ .
6. The last name of the first woman to win the Iditarod is ______ .
8. The first name of the woman who finished the Iditarod sixteen times is ______ .
9. Another word for **checkup** is ______ .

DOWN

1. In a ______ examination, nothing is overlooked.
2. Another word for **very wild** is ______ .
3. The planet that's between Mercury and Earth is ______ .
5. A great sled-dog race that's held in Alaska every year is called the ______ .
7. How many dogs are allowed on a team in the Iditarod?

GO TO PART C IN YOUR TEXTBOOK

Name _____

A INFORMATION ITEMS

1. The rules of the Iditarod state that every musher must rest for

   _____ hours at one checkpoint and must rest for

   _____ hours at two other checkpoints.

2. This rule was put in to protect the ▆▆▆▆ .
   - mushers
   - dogs
   - race officials

3. In what year was the first Iditarod?
   - 1973
   - 1963
   - 1993

4. During the first running of the Iditarod, how many dogs died during the race?
   - 10
   - 20
   - 30

5. During more recent years, how many dogs die during each race?
   - 5 to 8
   - 8 to 10
   - 2 to 3

B STORY ITEMS

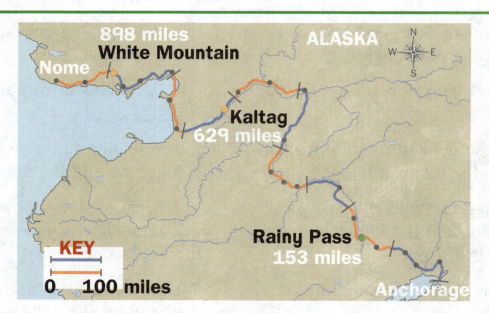

1. Make an **X** where Chad took his 24-hour rest stop.

2. Chad fell in the stream between checkpoint _____ and checkpoint _____ .

3. Something was the same around 150 miles of the race and around 600 miles of the race. What was that? _____

_____

4. What happened as the sled was going over a thick crust of frozen snow?

_____

5. Which dog let out a yelp? _____

6. Chad was in the water up to his _____ .

7. Name the 2 dogs that had to do most of the pulling to get the sled out of the water. _____

8. What did Chad do with the tarp? _____

9. What did Chad do first, take care of the injured dog or take care of himself?

_____

10. How much time did he have to get dry and warm? _____

11. What would have happened if he took too much time?

_____

12. Name **2** things he did inside the tent that he built.

_____

_____

13. What did Chad do to find the trail? _____

14. Whose sled did he see? _____

15. When he hitched the dogs to the gangline, which 2 dogs were the wheel dogs? _____

16. Which dog walked behind the sled? _____

17. Where was Chugger? _____

GO TO PART D IN YOUR TEXTBOOK

A STORY ITEMS

1. Where did Chad leave Chugger before going on to finish the race?

   _____

2. How many dogs were now on the gangline? _____

3. Which dog did not have a partner? _____

4. Chad finished the race in _____ th place.

5. Siri Carlson finished in _____ th place.

6. Did Chad meet his goal for this race? _____

7. What was that goal? _____

8. How did the mushers and their teams get back to Anchorage from Nome?

   _____

9. Who met Chad at the airport? _____

10. Susie had a lot of questions. Most of them were about _____ .

11. What had the vet told her the day before about Chugger?

    _____

    _____

12. What did Chad say he wanted to do with Denali for the next Iditarod?

    _____

13. Who did Chad plan to practice with during the summer?

    _____

14. Denali ran in six more Iditarods. Who was the musher for five of them?

    _____

15. Who was the other musher? _____

There's supposed to be a picture that shows the next chapter. Make a picture that shows the end of the story.

REVIEW ITEMS

1. Most sled-dog teams have an ▨▨▨▨ number of dogs.

   • even   • odd

2. For the Iditarod, a sled-dog team can't have more than _____ dogs.

3. Which letter in the picture shows the wheel dogs? _____

4. Which letter shows the swing dogs? _____

5. Which letter shows the lead dogs? _____

6. Which letter shows where the musher is most of the time? _____

7. Which letter shows tug lines? _____

8. Which letter shows the gangline? _____

Use these words to answer items 9–11:

   • swing dogs   • wheel dogs   • lead dogs

9. These dogs follow very well, and they are fast. _____

10. The important job of these dogs is to free the sled when it gets stuck.

   _____

11. These dogs are very smart, and other dogs obey them. _____

GO TO PART C IN YOUR TEXTBOOK

A | POEM ITEMS *A Lucky Thing*

Circle who is doing each thing.

1.	singing a melody	farmer	robin	chickens
2.	flinging grain	farmer	robin	chickens
3.	scratching the floor	farmer	robin	chickens
4.	latching the door	farmer	robin	chickens
5.	flying high	farmer	robin	chickens
6.	clucking	farmer	robin	chickens

B | PARTS OF A POEM

1. Each part of a poem is called a ▨ .

   • song   • story   • chapter   • stanza

2. *A Lucky Thing* has _____ stanzas.

3. *The New Kid* has _____ stanzas.

C | POEM ITEMS *The New Kid*

1. After the new kid arrived, the Tigers were on a ▨ streak.

   • losing   • winning

2. The full name of their baseball team is the _____

   _____ _____ .

3. In the last stanza of the poem, the author tells us that he and the other

   team members don't care that the new kid is ▨ .

   • a good player   • a poor player

   • a girl player   • a boy player

WRITING ABOUT POINT OF VIEW

Write about things that might make an animal look lucky to you but not to somebody else.

1. Think of an animal that you think is very lucky. Write a paragraph that tells why you think that animal is very lucky.

My Point of View

_____

_____

_____

_____

2. Write another paragraph about somebody who might think that animal is **not** very lucky. Tell about some of the things that make the animal unlucky.

Another Person's Point of View

_____

_____

_____

_____

END OF LESSON 100

Fact Game Scorecard Sheet

Fact Game for Test 6

1	2	3	4	5
6	7	8	9	10
11	12	13	14	15
16	17	18	19	20

Fact Game for Test 7

1	2	3	4	5
6	7	8	9	10
11	12	13	14	15
16	17	18	19	20

Fact Game for Test 8

1	2	3	4	5
6	7	8	9	10
11	12	13	14	15
16	17	18	19	20

Fact Game for Test 9

1	2	3	4	5
6	7	8	9	10
11	12	13	14	15
16	17	18	19	20

Fact Game for Test 10

1	2	3	4	5
6	7	8	9	10
11	12	13	14	15
16	17	18	19	20

Thermometer Chart

for Check 10 through Check 19

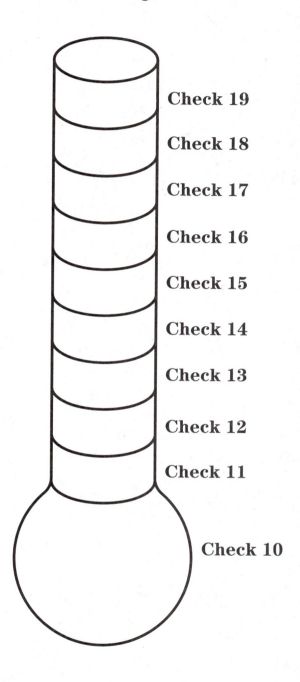

Check 19

Check 18

Check 17

Check 16

Check 15

Check 14

Check 13

Check 12

Check 11

Check 10